How to use this book

Follow the advice, in italics, given for you on each page.
Support the children as they read the text that is shaded in cream.
***Praise** the children at every step!*

Detailed guidance is provided in the Read Write Inc. Phonics Handbook

8 reading activities

Children:

- *Practise reading the speed sounds.*
- *Read the green and red words for the story.*
- *Listen as you read the introduction.*
- *Discuss the vocabulary check with you.*
- *Read the story.*
- *Re-read the story and discuss the 'questions to talk about'.*
- *Re-read the story with fluency and expression.*
- *Practise reading the speed words.*

Speed sounds

Consonants *Say the pure sounds (do not add 'uh').*

f ff	l ll	m mm	n nn kn	r rr	s ss	v ve	z zz s	sh	th	ng nk

b bb	c k ck	d dd	g gg	h	j	p **pp** (circled)	qu	t tt	w wh	x	y	ch tch

Vowels *Say the sounds in and out of order.*

at	hen head	in	on	up	day	see happy	high	blow

zoo	look	car	for door snore	fair	whirl	shout	boy

*Each box contains one sound but sometimes more than one grapheme. Focus graphemes are **circled**.*

Green words

Read in Fred Talk (pure sounds).

three stood smart arm far park star Mark

Margo Carl Clara go-kart car

Read the root word first and then with the ending.

start → starting lift → lifted

dart → darted end → ended stop → stopped

Red words

was to are old so go you the

Vocabulary check

Discuss the meaning (as used in the story) after the children have read each word.

	definition:
go-kart	*a cart built out of old bits of pram and junk*
sped	*went very fast*
starting post	*place where cars get ready to start the race*

Punctuation to note in this story:

Mark Margo Carl Clara	*Capital letters for names*
Three They The So	*Capital letters that start sentences*
.	*Full stop at the end of each sentence*
!	*Exclamation mark used to show anger*

Come on, Margo!

Introduction

Do you like cars? Do you like racing?
Does your mum/dad/brother/sister like racing?

The race you are going to read about is rather unusual. There are three very fast cars but there is also a rather odd looking go-kart driven by Margo. It doesn't seem likely that the go-kart can have any chance of winning.

Story written by Gill Munton
Illustrated by Tim Archbold

Three cars stood at the starting post.

Three smart cars - and an old go-kart!

The man lifted his arm to start them off.

They darted off along the track.

Vroom! Vroom!

Carl was in Car 1.

Clara was in Car 2.

Mark was in Car 3.

And Margo was in the go-kart.

The cars did not get far.

Car **1** ran off the track,

and ended up in the

car park.

So did Car **2**.

Car **3** - just stopped.

But look at that old go-kart!

You are a star, Margo!

Questions to talk about

Re-read the page. Read the question to the children. Tell them whether it is a **FIND IT** *question or* **PROVE IT** *question.*

FIND IT

✓ *Turn to the page*

✓ *Read the question*

✓ *Find the answer*

PROVE IT

✓ *Turn to the page*

✓ *Read the question*

✓ *Find your evidence*

✓ *Explain why*

Page 8:	FIND IT	*How many people were in the race?*
Page 8:	PROVE IT	*What do you think the go-kart driver is thinking as she waits to start?*
Page 9:	FIND IT	*How did the man start the race?*
Page 10-11:	FIND IT	*What are the names of all the drivers?*
Page 12:	FIND IT	*What happened to Car 1?*
Page 13:	FIND IT	*What happened to Car 2 and Car 3?*
Page 13:	PROVE IT	*Who won?*